Celeste T. Parker
Illustrated by Kimsey Pitts

A Division of Faith Books & MORE
Suwanee, GA

Beware of Bacon Bits
Copyright © 2011 Celeste T. Parker
All Rights Reserved.

Illustrated by Kimsey Pitts

No part of this publication may be reproduced, stored in a retrieval system, or transmitted in any form or by any means – electronic, mechanical, photocopying, recording, or otherwise - without the written permission of the author or publisher. The only exception is brief quotations in printed reviews.

First published by Friends of Faith™
ISBN 978-0-9846507-0-5

Printed in the United States of America.

This book is printed on acid-free paper.

A Division of Faith Books & MORE
3255 Lawrenceville-Suwanee Rd.
Suite P250
Suwanee, GA 30024
publishing@faithbooksandmore.com
www.faithbooksandmore.com

Dedication

**To Tony
For a love like no other**

Donation

In honor of my grandmother, Margaret McDowell, one dollar from each book sold will be donated to the American Cancer Society. Visit http://main.acsevents.org/goto/team_butterfly for more information.

Acknowledgements

Mom, thanks for all the "walks" we used to take: trips to the ballet, circus, concerts, movies, plays, restaurants—and for feeding my soul along the way.

Grandma, I know you are burning up the phone lines of heaven telling other angels about "Telesie's book" (smile). You are remembered still and loved always.

Sharon, thanks for traveling by plane, train, and automobile to support me (and do a little shopping, of course).

Dad, thanks for giving me advice on the business side, yet reminding me to have fun.

Delta Psi Epsilon Christian Sorority, Inc., thank you for reminding me who I am in Christ.

Zeta Phi Beta Sorority, Inc., thank you for embracing who I am and encouraging me to share God's gifts with the community. Life can be a blizzard, but your sisterly love keeps me warm.

Granville T. Woods Math & Science Academy, thanks for your overwhelming support and for "schooling" me. My experience with and service to you will always be dear to my heart.

Thank you, Heavenly Father, for so much more than a book. Thank you for purpose. Please take these books where you want them to go. Open the eyes, touch the hearts, and bless the lives of all who read them.

Letter to the Parents of Boys

Dear Reader,

Thank you for purchasing this book! Beware of Bacon Bits is similar to its literary sister, Pigs Don't Wear Pearls in that the main character is, and the theme still revolves around, a pig. This time, however, the pig has grown up and is now imparting wisdom to his son.

The story opens with a glimpse into the home of the Azurs (pronounced "as-you-are"). Bo Azur, Jr., (Boaz-you-are) has just turned ten and is wrestling with what can often be one's biggest foe, maturity. During a walk with his dad, he discovers that there is strength in weakness, that a life of significance is often one of sacrifice, and that we must eventually put away childish things.

Where Pigs Don't Wear Pearls dealt with the issue of purity, Beware of Bacon Bits encourages humility. It seeks to debunk the myth about what it really means to be a man. The world teaches that the measure of a man is the amount of physical strength, money, and women he possesses. The world has it backward. The Word, on the other hand, teaches that man was made in the image of G.O.D., not a d.o.g. Instead of being glory hogs, we are to acknowledge all gifts and successes as being from God and use them for His glory. The phrase, "bring home the bacon" means to succeed. A "bit" is defined as a small piece or amount or anything that curbs or restrains. It is my hope that boys will no longer settle for being less than who they are intended to be. It is my prayer that this work will open the door to talking to your sons, grandsons, nephews, brothers, and students about the prince that lies within.

Peace and blessings,
Celeste T. Parker

Letter to the Parents of Girls

Dear Reader,

Thank you for purchasing this book! Although the theme of Beware of Bacon Bits centers on a boy, I haven't forgotten my girls. Bo Jr., is learning that trying to fit society's mold of a man isn't cool. But there's a message for us females as well. When boys simply look our way it can sometimes give us "butterflies." This is a natural, God-given emotion. In the beginning, the first man identified with his job (taking care of the earth) while the woman identified with him (being his helper). Helper, however, does not mean helpless. God has given us our own gifts to open and share. The Bible warns against bad or nagging wives. I believe promiscuous and possessive girlfriends are their predecessors. We are not to spend our lives chasing or trying to outshine our counterparts. The earth needs and flourishes in our natural, God-given warmth and light.

In our various shades and sizes, we are gorgeous gems and fragrant flowers. Unlike real flowers, however, we have a choice whether or not to be plucked. We must stay rooted in spiritual soil, water ourselves with the Word, and in time, if God permits, love will blossom. Although boys and men can make life flavorful, they are not the main ingredient. What makes our lives sweet and complete is our relationship with Christ. It is my hope that boys and girls will respect one another despite media images to the contrary. I believe this starts with girls respecting themselves. It is my prayer that this work will open the door to talking to your daughters, granddaughters, nieces, sisters, and students about the pearl that lies within.

Peace and blessings,
Celeste T. Parker

Now that you are ten not two
You mustn't do
Things terrible.

I'll tell you what I mean
If you listen
To this parable.

Once there was a tiger
Who loved to lay
In sunshine

'Til the sun left the sky,
Thinking by and by
"One day he'll be all mine."

But the tiger
Liked to play in fields
With lush green grass and a lily

'Til he matured,
Grew self-assured,
And realized this was silly.

Looking toward the heavens
He observed
A butterfly,

But having gone through
change herself,
She kept on
Flying by.

Puzzled, he went on to say,
"With time, I've changed
My stripes."

But unconvinced,
She merely winced,
Remembering other similar types.

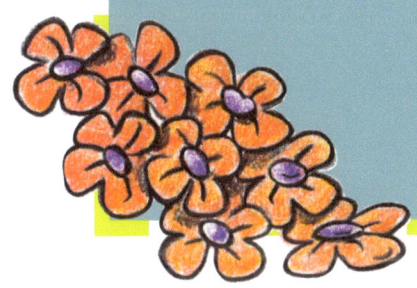

Seasons changed,
Feelings remained
And, in fact, grew intense

'Til her heart, too, fluttered,
Love like no other,
They've been together ever since.

Dad, that story's cool and all,
But we're not tigers,
WE...ARE...PIGS

Meant to be tough,
Built to be rough,
For dirty jobs,
not flowery gigs.

Well Bo,
It's meant to teach you
Others' lives you should not borrow

Lest your own should pass you by,
Seeds sown today
Bear fruit tomorrow.

Don't try to be
What you are not.
Avoid life's fiery pits.

You're more than a boar;
This truth don't ignore.
BEWARE OF BACON BITS!

"Don't be jealous or proud, but be humble and consider others more important than yourselves."

Philippians 2:3
Holy Bible,
Contemporary English Version